The VIP with Psychiatric Impairment

ALSO BY THE GROUP FOR THE ADVANCEMENT OF PSYCHIATRY

Normal Adolescence: Its Dynamics and Impact
(formulated by the Committee on Adolescence)

The Right to Abortion: A Psychiatric View
(formulated by the Committee on Psychiatry and Law)

Drug Misuse: A Psychiatric View of a Modern Dilemma
(formulated by the Committee on Mental Health Services)

The VIP with PSYCHIATRIC IMPAIRMENT

Formulated by the Committee on Governmental Agencies
GROUP FOR THE ADVANCEMENT OF PSYCHIATRY

CHARLES SCRIBNER'S SONS · NEW YORK

A-1.73(c)

Printed in the United States of America
Library of Congress Catalog Card Number 76-37208
SBN 684-12778-4 (cloth)
SBN 684-13259-1 (paper)

This report is dedicated to the memory of Robert T. Morse, M.D., a member of the Committee on Governmental Agencies until his untimely death in 1964. He was one of the first to suggest that the committee give the subject of this report careful, cautious, and considered study. Dr. Morse had an almost inexhaustible fund of information on the subject. He helped determine the direction that our deliberations took even after his death, and this report bears the impress of his thought.

STATEMENT OF PURPOSE

THE GROUP FOR THE ADVANCEMENT OF PSYCHIATRY has a membership of approximately three hundred psychiatrists, most of whom are organized in the form of a number of working committees. These committees direct their efforts toward the study of various aspects of psychiatry and the application of this knowledge to the fields of mental health and human relations.

Collaboration with specialists in other disciplines has been and is one of GAP's working principles. Since the formation of GAP in 1946 its members have worked closely with such other specialists as anthropologists, biologists, economists, statisticians, educators, lawyers, nurses, psychologists, sociologists, social workers, and experts in mass communication, philosophy, and semantics. GAP envisages a continuing program of work according to the following aims:

(1) To collect and appraise significant data in the field of psychiatry, mental health, and human relations;

(2) To re-evaluate old concepts and to develop and test new ones;
(3) To apply the knowledge thus obtained for the promotion of mental health and good human relations.

GAP is an independent group, and its reports represent the composite findings and opinions of its members only, guided by its many consultants.

The VIP with Psychiatric Impairment was formulated by the Committee on Governmental Agencies; the participation of former committee members and consultants is recognized in the Acknowledgments. The current members of this committee and all other committees of GAP are listed at the end of the book.

ACKNOWLEDGMENTS

THE COMMITTEE ON GOVERNMENTAL AGENCIES worked on this report for some ten years, first under the chairmanship of Donald B. Peterson, M.D., and later with Harold Rosen, M.D., as chairman. (The formulation of the report was completed under the leadership of Dr. Peterson.) During that period, the membership of the committee changed considerably. The following former members and consultants contributed significantly to the preparation of various drafts of this report and, in part, to its final phrasing.

Edward O. Harper, M.D., and Calvin S. Drayer, M.D., served on the committee during all its deliberations in formulating the report. Five other former members—Benjamin H. Balser, M.D., John M. Caldwell, M.D., Albert J. Glass, M.D., Edward J. Kollar, M.D., Norman Q. Brill, M.D.—served also as consultants. Three additional former members who served on the committee for four years until they requested transfer from active- to contributing-member status in GAP are William H. Anderson, M.D., Robert L. Williams, M.D., and Raymond W. Waggoner,

M.D., a recent past-president of the American Psychiatric Association.

All the consultants to the Committee on Governmental Agencies, some of them members of other GAP committees, gave freely of their time to the work of completing this study. The committee is especially indebted to Dexter M. Bullard, M.D., Paul F. Eggertsen, M.D., John P. Lambert, M.D., Zigmond M. Lebensohn, M.D., Hugh L'Etang, M.D., Victor F. Lief, M.D., Alan A. McClain, M.D., and Mottram P. Torre, M.D.

A number of officers in the armed forces of the United States also aided the committee in its work. Brigadier General S. L. A. Marshall, U.S. Army—Retired, served as a consultant, meeting with the committee at various times during the years of discussions and bringing a wealth of material to bear on the subject. Vice Admiral George G. Burkley, Medical Corps, USN, read the next-to-final draft of this report. The Chief Consultants in Psychiatry and Neurology, Office of the Surgeon General, for the Army, the Navy, and the Air Force, or their delegates, functioned as *ex-officio* consultants to the committee, meeting with it during all its sessions. The following officers served as consultants: Department of the Army—Colonel Bruce L. Livingston, Medical Corps, Colonel Matthew D. Parrish, Medical Corps, and Colonel William J. Tiffany, Jr., Medical Corps; Department of the Navy—Lieutenant Commander D. E. Brown, Medical Corps, and Captain R. L. Christy, Medical Corps; Department of the Air Force—Colonel Don E. Flinn, Medical Corps, and Colonel Paul Richards, USAF.

The committee is grateful to all the individuals who aided and supported its efforts to complete the work of formulating this report and bringing it to publication.

CONTENTS

The VIP with Psychiatric Impairment

INTRODUCTION: DEFINITIONS

THIS REPORT IS FOCUSED on the psychiatric implications of a major dilemma that permeates every organizational aspect of our society: the person in high position who is psychiatrically impaired.

The committee that formulated the report and its consultants were confronted in much of their work with a major problem. It stemmed from the fact that, because of the sensitive nature of this study, no pertinent factual clinical observations derived from actual contact with patients could be used. For obvious reasons we feel we cannot comment on contemporary or almost contemporary persons, a number of whom were the subject of the committee's discussions. The examples cited are largely anecdotal and are concerned for the most part with personages no longer living.

The definitions of the terms used in the title and contents of this report are intentionally broad. We wished to avoid any dispute over diagnostic terminology or about organic versus emotional causation. The definitions are:

VIP: "Very important person," a term coined by Sir Winston

Churchill, a person of considerable prestige or influence; especially, a high official receiving special privileges.

PSYCHIATRIC OR MENTAL IMPAIRMENT: Terms broadly used to describe a state of mind, whatever the cause, that is marked by disturbance of thinking, emotions, and behavior—or of one or another of these—so great as to affect adversely and to a significant degree the individual's performance as a leader.

We are concerned here solely with any degree of impairment that interferes with acceptable performance in the job. When degree of impairment and indications for treatment are considered, the psychiatric elements need to be evaluated. The VIP's total situation must be weighed. Social, political, and economic aspects are of prime significance, as are the effects that disturbing the equilibrium might have on both the VIP and the members of the group surrounding him.

one

THE VIP AND THE PSYCHIATRIST

GRAVE, PERHAPS INSUPERABLE, problems beset the process of making psychiatric evaluation and treatment available to a VIP whose mental functions have become impaired. His illness is disruptive to himself, to his group, and to society at large.

Since antiquity, society has been concerned with its leadership. Aristotle felt that officials should be men of character, capable of commanding the "passions" in situations where the public good is paramount.[1] Past tragedies clearly indicate that many unrecognized elements were at work between the leader and his followers.

The effective leader must use power wisely—or at least in a way the inner circle, the "in-group," considers wise—if his decisions in important matters are to continue to be accepted. If his intellectual capacity becomes impaired, he may be wholly unaware of the fact; because of his position as leader, close associates will emphasize his positive attributes and deny or hide any impairment of his capabilities, no matter how minor. The greater his authority, the fewer his intimate associates. The small group of "yes men" who cluster about the leader try to isolate him from any hostile criticism.

His advisers are keenly aware of how closely their careers are aligned with his. Through identification with him they derive status, influence, and power. At times, they use this relationship to establish goals and accomplish ends that may or may not be in accord with those of the VIP. The leader must mold his associates into a loyal, effective group, and this is impossible if mental illness has eroded his capacity for leadership.

How does an emotionally disturbed VIP get psychiatric help? For disease requiring medical or surgical treatment his closest associates speedily bring him the highest skills available, but, paradoxically, if he is adversely and significantly affected by psychic turmoil, the true nature of his disability is denied or distorted, and it becomes impossible for him to obtain even a modicum of the care he so desperately needs.

The military establishment can command its personnel to undergo medical, including psychiatric, examination. It is able to order even high-ranking personnel into a hospital. The military system is not—and by its very nature cannot be—democratic. It has devised procedures that do not ordinarily break down until the highest ranks are reached. But at that point they do break down. The judicial system tries to cope with the problem. So do churches and industries, and the professions. The U.S. State Department has a medical staff with part-time psychiatrists, but only in the career services can problem-solving techniques be pragmatically applied, and, again, these procedures break down at the highest levels. It is lamentable and indeed tragic that the emotionally disturbed VIP does not get the help his condition requires. How can the psychiatrist function if a head of state is affected? If a president, prime minister, or king is paranoid but the inner circle nevertheless judges him effective, its members dismiss his paranoid behavior as "merely eccentric" or simply characterize him as "difficult." If he is aging or senile the problem may be less complicated. If he is depressed, has mood swings, and is suicidal or homicidal, a psychiatrist usually is not consulted.

The examining psychiatrist's responsibility is the same as that of any other consultant physician: to arrive at an accurate diagnosis and to make recommendations for treatment. But he can neither make nor enforce a decision. He serves as a consultant—that is, in an advisory capacity—to increase understanding of the VIP in order to determine if treatment is indicated and, if so, to recommend how and under what conditions it can best proceed.

A degree of aberrant behavior in a leader may be helpful. John Brown's grandiose bearing strengthened his followers. General George Patton's impetuosity may have helped him accomplish some of his military feats. Before Yorktown, George Washington, perhaps with cause, was often depressed by a conviction that the Revolution would fail. Yet he persisted in efforts to overcome adverse forces and ultimately led the Continental Army to victory. On the other hand, as Benito Mussolini came to realize he had brought Italy to the verge of ruin, he lost his sense of humor, became indecisive, procrastinated, and impulsively made a number of bizarre, ineffective decisions that alienated even some of his closest associates.[2]

The question of whether creativity or productivity in a political figure is impaired is unique. When, for instance, should a leader be relieved? Psychopathology does not *per se* imply decreased or impaired effectiveness. The problem is to decide when limits need to be imposed, what the limits should be, and how they should be imposed.

The psychiatrist does not have all the answers. He may not have any. But he can at times—although only at times—state why a particular VIP acts and reacts the way he does. He may not be able to speak in terms of diagnosis. He can refuse to make predictions. Recommendations may or may not be possible. If necessary, a board of psychiatrists can be called upon to make formal predictions and recommendations.

No physician can make or enforce decisions; this is not a physician's role. If a President of the United States were to develop cancer of the bowel, how could he be forced to undergo surgery? Yet bodily illness is not stigmatized in the way mental disease—actual, potential, or suspected—is.

Who are the physicians, internists, surgeons, and psychiatrists who find themselves in the position of examining eminent leaders? A political figure is always oriented in a given direction. So are his appointees. In the political arena we can expect to find physicians of appropriate political persuasion. Physicians may be part of the VIP's entourage. Will the psychiatrist who is requested to examine a high-level VIP be so appointed because of his own position? For example, the president of a royal academy of medicine will usually become his king's physician. Highly competent practitioners have been appointed in the past, but so have individuals who condoned incapacity, some of whom enjoyed manipulating persons and situations, and some of whom, in the words of Hugh L'Etang, while basking in reflected glory, have played God.[3] The Nazis and their "research" physicians are prime examples.

Can boards instead of individuals be appointed in advance to deal with the problem of psychiatric impairment in VIPs? How can medical integrity be preserved and confidentiality maintained without penalizing the larger group? This is an ever-present national and international social problem. Some tentative recommendations for solutions are listed in Chapter seven.

There are no easy answers, but society must find answers of some kind. Former solutions are becoming untenable. Future failures may be catastrophic.

two EMOTIONALLY ILL VIPS IN HISTORY

HISTORY IS REPLETE with examples of mentally impaired VIPs. Vignettes of a few which are relatively recent reveal their characteristics and those of their close associates, as well as the consequences of the impairment, attitudes and actions, and the various methods used in dealing with the problems. King George III of England; King Ludwig II of Bavaria; President Hindenburg of Germany; Benito Mussolini, Il Duce, of Italy; and, in the United States, Presidents Woodrow Wilson and Franklin D. Roosevelt, Governor Earl Long, and Secretary of Defense James V. Forrestal illustrate these with the sharpness of caricature.

George III, King of England

George III, king of England from 1760 to 1820, had five episodes of major mental impairment during his reign. They were marked by unpredictable, unrealistic decisions in affairs of state which splintered his relationships with his family, his physicians, his cabinet, and Parliament. Efforts to conceal his disturbed behavior were fruitless, although these extended to purchasing and suppressing a published history. The party in power wished to retain a *status quo* that included the "mad king," but the opposition, which wanted a regency, finally prevailed. Mental impairment in this VIP, probably due to porphyria,[1] a disease of faulty metabolism in which such episodes may occur, contributed significantly to reversing the entire power structure of England.

Ludwig II, King of Bavaria

Ludwig II, king of Bavaria (1846–1886), the "fairy-tale king," was a highly intelligent patron of the arts and during the early years of his reign demonstrated considerable capability in affairs of government. His paranoia increasingly impaired his effectiveness; he spent more and longer periods of time secluded in remote castles, neglected his governmental duties, and became increasingly suspicious of others. According to one biographer, Ludwig's youthful dislike of human society developed into contempt for the whole human race.[2] Anything to do with women involved him in an alien, inaccessible world. His path was the path of furious solitude.

After he ran out of personal funds for his feverish castle-building program, he diverted state funds to it and sought foreign loans for the project. He estranged former supporters, the public, the ministry, and his own family. But only when his plans meant ruin for too many did it become feasible to remove him from office. On June 8, 1886, a panel of psychiatrists reported that he had paranoia. The cabinet and the prime minister took drastic action, declared a regency two days later, and appointed a commission of cabinet officers and psychiatrists to inform Ludwig that he was suspended from office and that they were taking him into custody. Ludwig promptly ordered their arrest. Members of his household and people in the village had not regarded him as mentally ill until he ordered his captives skinned alive.[3] The commission was released and Ludwig was taken to Schloss Berg, a castle equipped for his care and treatment. However, presumably because of his status, the usual precautions in caring for a dangerous paranoid patient were relaxed. He was later found dead from drowning, along with a psychiatrist on the commission, in the Starnberger See, a lake near the castle.

Paul von Hindenburg

The case of Hindenburg (1847–1934) illustrates how a man of undistinguished intellectual attainments can gain prominence as a symbol and maintain this position even after senility develops. A typical Junker aristocrat, Paul von Beneckendorff und Hindenburg made the army his career until he was retired from command of a corps in 1911. Early in World War I, Germany's Eastern Front almost collapsed. General Erich Ludendorff (1865–1937), who had distinguished himself at Liège, was called from the Western Front to stop the Russian threat in the east. Ludendorff, however, was a commoner, and a titled commanding officer was traditional. Up to this point Hindenburg had been virtually unknown. Yet at sixty-seven, he was pulled out of retirement into the limelight, in which he remained until he died twenty years later.

His career was characterized by faltering reluctance to face issues squarely and by evasion of responsibility at critical moments. After the Battle of Tannenberg (August 25–30, 1914), "in the eyes of the public the savior of East Prussia was the nominal commander, Hindenburg. The elderly general . . . was transformed into a titan by the victory. The triumph in East Prussia, lauded and heralded beyond its true proportions, fastened the Hindenburg myth upon Germany." [4] In 1925, when Friedrich Ebert, the first president of the Weimar Republic, died, Hindenburg was again called out of retirement. Following his election to the presidency, his mediocrity gradually became aggravated by senility that left him totally unprepared to deal with any degree of effectiveness with the turmoil in Germany during the early 1930s and with Hitler's drive for power.

By June 1932, the "political power of Germany no longer resided, as it had since the birth of the Republic, in the people and in the body which expressed the people's will, the Reichstag. It was now concentrated in the hands of a senile, eighty-five-year-old president and in those of a few shallow ambitious men around him who shaped his weary, wandering mind. Hitler saw this very clearly, and it suited his purposes." [5]

After Hindenburg's death it was possible to point out that he had never achieved true greatness. He was largely responsible for Germany's losing World War I and for the fact that she continued to fight long after defeat was inevitable. He was a monarchist through and through, who could not logically have been expected to be a true servant of the Republic, although he had taken an oath on the Constitution. He was of mediocre intelligence and boasted that he had read no more than six books in his life.[6] Yet this man was allowed to retain the power that enabled him to appoint Adolf Hitler Chancellor of Germany on January 30, 1933.[7]

Woodrow Wilson

President Woodrow Wilson (1856–1924) was a stable, successful leader who became mentally impaired while in office. His brilliant, disciplined, incisive mind, blunted by progressive arteriosclerotic brain disease, was unable to cope with the pressing problems of the peace following World War I. From the time of a cerebrovascular accident on September 26, 1919, until his term expired on March 4, 1921, there was significant and progressive reduction in his working capacity and his ability to grasp problems at hand. After waiting three months to see the President, Viscount Grey, the British Ambassador, was neither received nor accredited and chose to return to England without even seeing Wilson about important international affairs. Subsequently other ambassadors were accredited without his receiving them. A great many bills automatically became law without the President's signature.

After the onset of his illness Wilson broke with such key men in his administration as Colonel Edward M. House, Secretary of State Robert Lansing, and Joseph Tumulty, his private secretary, close friend, and political adviser. His dependence on his wife became intense. Mrs. Wilson, who had no formal education after the age of twelve, received and sent official messages and often decided not only who should see the President but what subjects should be discussed. Thus shielded, he was unable to recognize the stirrings in the Senate and the adverse public opinion in regard to the Treaty of Versailles. "I studied every paper, sent from the different Secretaries or Senators," Mrs. Wilson stated, but "I, myself, never made a single decision regarding the disposition of public affairs. The only decision that was mine was as to what was important and what was not, and . . . when to present matters to my husband." [8] Accordingly, the President could not receive full or timely information about vital problems affecting the nation.

At first Wilson directed that his condition remain secret. Physicians issued evasive statements. Some leading physicians advised Mrs. Wilson that recovery might come quickly and without aftereffects.[9] These and other aspects of the situation are covered in a sympathetic and scholarly book, *When the Cheering Stopped* by Gene Smith, which gives a frightening exposition of those times, events, and personalities. Wilson quickly rejected anyone suspected of disloyalty. Because he had the power to give or withhold patronage, to veto bills, and to control the Democratic Convention, his followers could not risk loss of personal status by breaking with him.

"Secretary of State Lansing, however, believed that Wilson was incapacitated and proposed that the President be relieved of office," wrote Cary Grayson, Wilson's personal physician. "He was unable to move because Wilson's physicians insisted the President would recover, and because no machinery for removal from office short of impeachment existed. Thus, the incapacitated Wilson remained in a position of power which he could not exercise constructively. The high regard of the populace for the beloved and respected leader is neither easily nor quickly shaken. So it was that in one of the most significant periods in the history of our country, none dared to run counter to a determined leader whose impairment of intellectual function had robbed him of the very qualities that made him revered throughout the world." [10]

Franklin D. Roosevelt

President Franklin D. Roosevelt (1882–1945) died on April 12, 1945, at the age of sixty-three, fifteen weeks after the crucial Yalta conference on February 2 of that year. William C. Bullitt, former U.S. Ambassador to the Soviet Union, declared that "at Yalta Roosevelt was more than tired, he was ill." [11] John Gunther stated that on the voyage from Yalta "Roosevelt's fatigue was crushing and he had intermittent periods of being virtually comatose." [12] Sir Winston Churchill described Roosevelt as frail and ill on the eve of the Yalta Conference.

These are statements of lay, not medical, people. Churchill was defending a position at variance with the one taken by Roosevelt. All observers present were biased to some degree, but it seems significant that their observations were congruent.

By February 27, 1945, the Russians were on their way toward Berlin. According to Churchill's later writings about this period, "Roosevelt's health and strength had faded. In my long telegrams I thought I was talking to my trusted friend . . . as I had done all these years . . . [However his] devoted aides . . . drafted in combination the answers which were sent in his name. . . . Roosevelt could only give general guidance and approval." (Such telegrams are normally drafted by the staff: Churchill implies that Roosevelt was unable to provide much guidance.) ". . . And Harry Hopkins [Roosevelt's special assistant], who might have given personal help, was himself seriously ailing. . . ." Churchill received a cable from the President on April 11, the day before his death.[13]

Churchill has described the ultimate dilemma well: "We can now see the deadly hiatus which existed between the fading President Roosevelt's strength and the growth of President Truman's grip of the vast world problem. In this melancholy void one President could not act, and the other could not know. Neither the military chiefs nor the State Department received the guidance they required, and the indispensable political direction was lacking at the moment when it was most needed." [14]

Further insight into Roosevelt's mental state during this period is given by Robert Murphy, who was political adviser to General Dwight D. Eisenhower and scheduled to be the ranking State Department representative in Occupied Germany. Summoned to Washington for urgent consultations, Murphy later characterized Roosevelt as in no condition to offer balanced judgments upon major issues, so that the Army during this period was making decisions that the civilian authority of the Government would normally make.[15]

A contrary opinion is offered by Rear Admiral Ross T. McIntire, Surgeon General of the Navy and personal physician to President Roosevelt from 1933 until the President's death. He presented substantial medical evidence based on his own examinations and those of carefully selected medical consultants that the President's condition was essentially normal except for extreme fatigue; that Roosevelt's fatal, massive cerebral hemorrhage could not have been predicted; and that the only significant medical problem was the one associated with Roosevelt's occasional upper respiratory infections and the excessive fatigue brought on by his herculean efforts to do so much himself. McIntire reported that at no time did he show any mental impairment.[16]

Whether Roosevelt's judgment and effectiveness at the Yalta Conference were impaired by organic brain disease preceding his death from a massive cerebral hemorrhage is the subject of a continuing debate that is unlikely ever to be settled. In March 1944, Howard G. Bruenn, M.D., was called to examine the President and found hypertension, hypertensive heart disease, and cardiac failure. During the nine years from 1935, Roosevelt's blood pressure had risen from 136/78 to 186/108. His condition responded to digitalization and some curtailment of physical activity.[17] The historian James MacGregor Burns states: "On the face of it, Bruenn's findings would seem to support the charge that Roosevelt was an ill man at Yalta, and, indeed, during the last year or two of his life. Paradoxically, Bruenn's disclosures . . . will force us to revise most interpretations of the significance of Roosevelt's medical condition during his final year. For Bruenn's records indicate that during the last year the digitalis and other ministrations seemed to work."[18]

Since the men under consideration here are from recent history, such barriers to understanding as loss of records, semantic difficulty, and unfamiliarity with the culture might be expected to be at a minimum. But complete medical records of a VIP are seldom obtainable. For instance, one neurologist who examined Wilson directed that all records of his examinations be destroyed on his death to preserve their confidentiality.

Descriptive comments are of course available from reporters, but reporters are lay observers who also may be biased. Some identify with the leader's policies and therefore defend and justify them; others defend policies of their own that are at variance with those of the VIP in question. Gunther's, Murphy's, and Churchill's comments must be evaluated from the same standpoint. But so must those of McIntire, a physician but not a psychiatrist. Beyond doubt, any individual reporting and recording such data lacks complete information, and the correctness of his evaluation is limited not only by his own bias but also by the extent of his field of competence.

Churchill's comment on Harry Hopkins's illness shows the importance of the confidant, a person of real VIP status, although of a secondary order. As a leader becomes increasingly more powerful, he may become increasingly surrounded, as the psychiatrist Lester Grinspoon states, "by a tight-knit group of deferential subordinates whose interests are often best served by pleasing and impressing him and who are careful about how they disagree with him." [19] As the group with which the leader routinely associates contracts, he may feel an increasing sense of loneliness. The ability of family and close friends to relieve this loneliness may be reduced as he becomes increasingly absorbed in problems he may not share with them because of their technicality or their security aspects. The leader may develop a relationship with some one person to whom he can talk freely, but he may come to overvalue this relationship, and its loss, should it end, may be extremely difficult to bear. The higher the position of the leader, the more exaggerated these changes may become. As he rises to positions where his decisions influence greater and greater numbers of people, he becomes increasingly isolated from them, and as he becomes increasingly well known he becomes lonelier.[20] Hopkins's illness at a critical period in affairs of state deprived both Roosevelt and Churchill of a trusted confidant.

Benito Mussolini

Under certain conditions, followers of a charismatic leader attempt to preserve the father image, following him unconditionally without asking why, even after his image has begun to tarnish. This was the case, even after his death, with the Italian dictator Benito Mussolini (1883–1945). One of the members of our committee was a U.S. Army medical officer in Italy at the time Mussolini died. This officer obtained a block of Il Duce's brain tissue from C. Mario Cattabeni, M.D., coroner of Milan, who performed the autopsy on Mussolini's body.[21] To secure it, he signed an agreement with the Committee of Liberation of Northern Italy "for the Surgeon, Fifth Army" in which he guaranteed that all findings would be kept strictly confidential. There would be no announcement of any pathology discovered on study of the tissue.[22] Sections were prepared and examined in Naples by the 15th General Medical Laboratory and in Washington by pathologists at the Army Medical Museum. From the very beginning, the Italian civil authority, whose Resistance associates had just killed Mussolini, judged the question from a nationalistic standpoint. When a request for access to Dr. Cattabeni's microscopic findings was made by the Americans in 1962, they found that special permission of the Italian government was required; this would be granted "under conditions specified by the Italian authorities." [23] The microscopic findings were never released. Italian nationalist tradition, rather than differences in political philosophy, seems to have been paramount.

three

PROBLEMS OF COPING WITH MENTAL IMPAIRMENT

EXAMPLES OF VIPs who have remained or been retained in office despite gross impairment can be drawn from government, the military, the judiciary, industry, the church—in fact from every area of public life. Effective procedures for introducing therapy appropriate to their special situations are nonexistent. Furthermore, procedures both to introduce treatment and to transfer powers and functions of the VIP must necessarily be improvised. They are usually unsuccessful.

Earl K. Long

In 1959, despite the combined efforts of family, friends, and state officials, Governor Earl K. Long (1895–1959) of Louisiana did not receive anything remotely approximating satisfactory treatment nor was it possible to make suitable arrangements for the orderly transfer of his duties during the period of his illness. None of the members of the committee that formulated this report saw or examined him, and we are in no position to assess the damage to government or individuals that may have been occasioned by his mental impairment. Its severity, however, is implicit in published statements such as this one: "At the end of the session, the legislators hurried off like conspirators. Filled with fear over what political secrets he might reveal, and demoralized by his personal insults," they took measures for speedy adjournment.[1]

Governor Long removed from office several high-ranking officials, including the State Director of Hospitals, for having participated in the effort to hospitalize him. Apparently there existed no legal means to transfer or abridge his functions and his powers, as long as he remained alive and stayed physically within the boundaries of his state. An attempt had been made earlier to provide definitive therapy outside Louisiana, but this failed. The Governor thereafter circumvented commitment to a Louisiana state hospital by calling a meeting of the State Hospital Board, which he controlled; the board relieved the Acting Superintendent of the hospital and granted legal authority to exercise psychiatric decision to a general practitioner, who had the Governor released without a sanity hearing.

Commitment laws recognize the fact that some mentally impaired people lack the necessary insight to cooperate in a voluntary treatment plan. When the individual is above the law or can manipulate it, any legal procedure is impotent.

James V. Forrestal

A definitive study of Secretary of Defense James V. Forrestal (1892–1949) by the political scientist Arnold A. Rogow emphasizes the extent to which close associates failed to realize Forrestal's mental condition was anything other than a state of fatigue.[2] They rejected all contrary viewpoints. They were convinced that he was mentally ill only after he presented what they could accept as alarming symptoms. Then, but only then, he received appropriate psychiatric attention. Innumerable administrative complexities and interference from various political, military, and church sources contributed to the difficulties of providing him with good psychiatric care. He was suffering from a severe depressive illness that eventually led to his suicide.

Military Personnel

Both fictionalized and factual examples are available to illustrate problems related to mental illness in commissioned personnel of modest social position in private life who achieved VIP status while in command at sea.[3] The military has specific procedures for coping with mental illness in all ranks, but their application to persons with VIP rank is beset with difficulty. The services authorize and require periodic medical evaluation of officers and special evaluation of any or all personnel as circumstances warrant. The decision for this rests with the commanding officer. He may be advised by medical or other officers of his command, or regulations for special assignment may require evaluation of an individual's reliability. Upon referral the psychiatrist (or other medical examiner) must assess the officer's physical and mental fitness to remain on duty or in some especially sensitive assignment. In effect, physicians are supposed to consider the physical and mental condition of the individual officer with respect to the general and specific requirements of his position. If he is not qualified for the position, he may be referred for appropriate treatment, returned to duty with specific limitations, retired, or discharged. But high-enough rank makes evaluation of this type with appropriate action difficult if not impossible.

A relatively contemporary and therefore unnamed commander of a large military medical unit came to official attention when the regular officer chiefs of several of his professional services submitted resignations because of his alleged unpredictable and abusive behavior, stating that he flew into tantrums at fancied slights and manifested angry uncalled-for behavior in the civilian community. He refused to greet a civilian psychiatric consultant during a routine visit and attempted to avoid conversation with him. When this was forced, he appeared manic, suspicious, and delusional, and displayed distorted concepts of reality. At the recommendation of the consultant to the Surgeon General, this officer was relieved of his duties and transferred to a general hospital for definitive diagnosis and treatment.

Significantly, in this case, local personnel were unable to cope with the situation without the intervention of an outside consultant from a higher echelon. But such an outside consultant could be obtained, and the commander, unlike Governor Long, could not negate his recommendations. With high-enough rank, however, the system, as has been mentioned, does break down. And it can malfunction for other reasons.

In an overseas installation, a young, inexperienced medical officer with only a few months of psychiatric training, noticed that his commander was often erratic and irritable, bombastic, demanding, and unpredictable when dealing with subordinates. At times he would place unreasonable demands upon them; at other times, he would pay little or no attention to problems of command. Gradually officers of his command discreetly reported his unusual behavior to the medical officer. They painted a picture of the commander that closely resembled Captain Queeg in Herman Wouk's novel, *The Caine Mutiny*. The medical officer also became increasingly aware of inappropriate behavior in the commander's dealings with officials of the host government. He seemed contemptuous of the country's people and culture and openly ridiculed local customs. His personal dress was flamboyant and his behavior overbearing. The American ambassador became concerned. He felt that the commander was jeopardizing friendly relationships with the host country. The medical officer agreed that the commander was much too mentally disturbed to carry out his duties.

But the usual channels of communication to higher headquarters were not open, since the commander could stop all messages and thereby not only prevent appropriate investigation and action but almost certainly institute reprisals. At the request of the ambassador, the medical officer prepared a report and sent it to the Surgeon General through diplomatic channels, using maximum security measures.

On reviewing the report the Surgeon General's psychiatric consultant concluded that the commander might be mentally ill but had doubts as to the credibility of the information. Was an inexperienced medical officer overreacting to reports from subordinate officers who disliked the commander, or even to his own relationship with the latter? Could the entire report represent the delusions of a mentally ill doctor? No member of the Surgeon

General's staff knew the physician personally. There was no doubt, however, about the ambassador's expressed concern. The consultant therefore recommended special medical evaluation of the commander under conditions of the utmost discretion to protect both commander and doctor. As few personnel as possible were to be involved. Unfortunately, Murphy's Law—which states, in essence, that if anything is so designed that it can fail, sooner or later it will—prevailed. The entire correspondence was returned through routine military channels, from Washington through each intermediate headquarters to the commander himself, spreading this information among hundreds of people and violating all arrangements for secrecy. In the turmoil that followed, no action was taken to determine whether the commander was actually sick or not. The young medical officer was transferred, and the ambassador became embittered over this breach of trust, for which he justifiably blamed the medical and military services.

This is a prime example of failure to implement an apparently well-structured system. Paranoid situations and paranoid officers can sometimes be treated with a minimum of red tape but sometimes, for administrative or other reasons, they may be untreatable.[4] No regulation of the armed forces authorizes a medical officer to require anyone not already under his care to submit to an examination. Such an order must be given by a superior in the chain of command. The higher his rank and the more responsible his job, the more harm an emotionally sick officer can do—and the more damage a medical officer's error can cause. The armed forces deprive a patient of command authority during hospitalization, but the VIP officer often seems not to have been apprised of this.

Members of the Judiciary

Psychiatric impairment in the judiciary needs also to be considered. This is another example of a hierarchy, less structured than the military, traditionally with virtually no formal policing of its membership's health from either within or without. In addition to the type of VIP problems already discussed, judges realize that previous decisions or rulings may be challenged if it becomes public knowledge that a judge's mental powers have in any way been impaired. Various attempts have been made in several states to deal with the problem of the incompetent judge. In discussing these, J. E. Frankel, executive secretary of the California Bar Association, comments:

"Leaving the decision to the judge himself or to the electorate is naive. The traditional measures of impeachment redress have failed. Compulsory retirement at a fixed age is limited at best, besides introducing other objections. Permitting action to remove judges convicted of a crime is obviously of narrow application." [5] Elimination by executive action has been avoided to insure freedom for the judiciary from executive control.

Some states, for example Ohio and Wisconsin, have grievance committees to consider complaints of judicial misconduct, and the problem therefore becomes that of discipline by the bar. But are committees of lawyers competent or even able to function in this way? Can or should a bar organization assume primary responsibility for recognizing mental impairment in a member of the judiciary? Will lawyers present and try charges against the very judges before whom they are or soon may be defending clients or waging suit?

In Texas, according to Frankel, the Supreme Court may act against a District Court judge on written presentation under oath by ten lawyers practicing in that judge's court. The Louisiana Supreme Court may try judges for misconduct on suit by its attorney general at the governor's request, or on request by twenty-five citizens and taxpayers or by one-half of all the attorneys in the judge's district. The Alabama Supreme Court may remove a judge (except a Supreme Court judge) for cause after charges are specified by the attorney general or by five taxpayers in the judge's district. In Michigan, the Supreme Court can initiate investigations, and recommend (to the governor or the state legislature) the removal of a jurist. New York has a Court on the Judiciary which sends notice of charges against a judge and the date of his trial to the governor, the president of the Senate, and the Speaker of the Assembly. But if a member of the state legislature prefers the same charges in the legislature, the judge need not answer in the Court on the Judiciary, and its proceedings are then stayed pending legislative determination.

According to Frankel, "the model judiciary article for State constitutions endorsed by the American Bar Association provides that, except for Supreme Court justices (subject to removal only by impeachment), all judges shall be subjected to retirement for incapacity and to removal for cause by the Supreme Court after hearing." [6]

In 1960, the California electorate by a large majority established a Judicial Qualifications Commission to deal with lack of fitness in judges. This commission has the authority to investigate and proceed against any California judge if there may have been willful misconduct in office, willful and persistent failure to perform his duty, habitual intemperance, or any permanent disability seriously interfering with the performance of his duties. After appropriate preliminaries, the commission may recommend to the State Supreme Court the removal or retirement of the judge, although in actual practice judges under inquiry or investigation apparently tend to retire or resign rather than face removal action.

Of the first ten cases resulting in retirement or resignation, three separations were due to impaired mental condition, including such signs as instability, failing memory, inability to concentrate and comprehend, and patterns of erratic and perverse behavior.

No legal procedure exists for the forced retirement or removal of a justice of the Supreme Court of the United States if the only issue were that he had become impaired while in office. An informal procedure has evolved in which, by agreement among the other justices, decisions are not handed down in cases in which the vote of an impaired justice is pivotal. At some point, when impairment becomes severe, the others recommend to the justice that he retire. This procedure seems to have been effective.

VIPs in Industry, the Church, and Other Organizations

In industry, religious establishments, and all other organizations in which leaders acquire a high degree of power, the same problems exist. There is no need to multiply examples, since the principles and underlying circumstances have been covered in the preceding discussion.

four PSYCHIATRIC DETERMINATION OF RELIABILITY, JUDGMENT, AND COMPETENCE

THE PSYCHIATRIST TODAY finds himself holding a concept of mental illness somewhere between the traditional "individual" model and the new, more generalized "systems" model.

The traditional medical individual model of mental illness recognizes a variety of disorders in which the disturbed behavior may be due to a disease process in the patient's body (or mind). Often the disturbed behavior may be an expression of an overwhelming emotional stress or inner conflict. The syndrome of symptoms, characteristic of the disorder, is labeled with a diagnosis. Treatment now is not always a straightforward agreement between doctor and patient. Meeting the requirements of a third party—whether a financial payer such as an insurance carrier or, in the case of a VIP, the group around him—can be a prerequisite to effective treatment.

The "systems" model considers the individual and his symptoms as part of communication within a social system, such as an official staff, a family, or a military unit. The individual may be seen as playing a symptomatic role that his group needs. Individual diagnosis, once stated or publicized, may cause a stigma which immediately effects a change in social relationships, or it may constitute a self-fulfilling prophecy, thereby becoming part of treatment rather than merely of evaluation.

Intervention necessarily affects the group's life course. It likewise affects the psychiatrist either as a private practitioner and consultant or as a responsible member of the staff. In the military, the psychiatrist does not have command responsibility, but he nevertheless has inescapable staff responsibility when he states that specific group-disturbing behavior is not due to medical (as contrasted to psychiatric) disease. He is expected to contribute his opinions to staff thinking. And the group pays the psychiatrist just as it pays any other permanent or consulting member on its staff.

In his routine work, the psychiatrist ideally makes an independent value judgment regarding the reliability of data and the statements of his patient. At some levels his opinions about judgment and over-all competence are regarded only as educated personal opinions to be accepted or rejected by a judge or jury. Psychiatrists tend to feel offended by this, because they view themselves as competent by virtue of training and experience to evaluate judgmental capacities of individuals in the same sense that an internist considers himself able to determine the normality of heart sounds, or a surgeon the presence of an operable lesion. Surgeons and internists, however, are rarely called upon to justify their findings: these are usually accepted without question, and if questioned can usually be justified. But many laymen consider themselves as competent as any psychiatrist to evaluate an individual's judgment. The law maintains its prerogative of deciding when and if the judgment and competence of a specific individual is adequate, and whether he must be considered responsible for his actions.

The psychiatrist can bring to his mental examination of a patient an objective attitude, a scientific approach, sound technical knowledge, special examination techniques, and a broad background of experience. He is best able to relate the quality of judgment to other aspects of personality, intelligence, mood, disorder of thought, and general medical disability.

These qualifications give the psychiatrist a special standing in court cases. But while his opinion may be sought, it is not necessarily accepted *in toto.* A court is often confronted by seemingly divergent and opposing opinions advanced by two psychiatrists who are equally well qualified. These differences are often more apparent than real; they are emphasized by the adversary system of trial in which prosecution and defense are both entitled to stress whatever part of the total potential testimony each considers favorable to its cause. There is much less disagreement where court procedures allow a greater latitude of testimony.

Psychiatrists must realize that their opinions about competence, reliability, and judgment are not always accepted by laymen, or, for that matter, by other psychiatrists. There are no precise, graduated scales of these capacities. In fact, evaluation of judgment and competence has different applications from person to person and place to place and perhaps even with the same person at slightly different times, but these qualities should always be evaluated with respect to the specific functions expected of the individual in the position he occupies. With VIPs at the higher levels, there are particular factors that tend to make this goal unattainable.

five SIGNIFICANT ASPECTS OF THE VIP SITUATION

THE LEADER IS SIGNIFICANT as a symbol. Furthermore, members of the in-group tend to try to maintain the existing power structure. (Count Galeazzo Ciano ultimately paid with his life for doing otherwise in opposing Mussolini.) For these two reasons the associates of a VIP conceal the weaknesses of their leader from public view to the point of blocking diagnosis and effective care if he becomes emotionally ill. In certain critical situations such tactics may be a *sine qua non* for the continuance of the power structure, but they are used even when no untoward political turbulence would probably result from transfer of authority. Not even a dictator would be able to circumvent adequate medical management of illness if his political associates all cooperated in a suitable plan. They rarely do. Competence to perform a job or hold political office is generally considered not a medical question but a matter of social judgment. Paranoid thinking may be labeled merely eccentric. Many leaders possess personality attributes that even specific members of the in-group find questionable or objectionable. Such traits are often part of the stamp of the leader, are useful in furthering group or national purpose or solidarity, and, so long as they do not interfere with decision-making, are not themselves evidence of mental illness. The state of a VIP's health is one factor on which group decisions are based, but it is only one. A physician may be brought in if treatment appears likely to further the in-group's interests or if the individual VIP himself seeks it.

Persons who have attained high position tend to believe they understand the over-all picture in a way impossible for anyone of lesser attainment. They cannot ascribe credibility to the findings of anyone with a less global breadth of vision. The responsibility and the standards for evaluating the current mental competence of a VIP are poorly defined. In the legislative branch of government, for example, the rest of the members of the legislative body constitute the evaluating group for one of their number; sometimes the total electorate does. But large groups have difficulty in agreeing that a problem even exists. They are unable to assess and evaluate medical information even when it is available. Governor Earl Long was elected to Congress even though his mental condition had been highlighted by press, radio, and television during the closing phase of his governorship. (He died before he could actually take his seat in Congress.) The fact that a VIP is mentally impaired is merely one consideration among many. Should anything be done about it? If so, what? Only advice from another VIP may seem credible to the members of the in-group, for only a VIP, they may feel, can understand.

One of the most significant factors is class solidarity. Individuals with common backgrounds and interests tend to defend or "cover for" one another. Insofar as possible, members of groups—military officers, churchmen, legislators, business executives, professional associates—for obvious reasons avoid active evaluation by one another, let alone by juniors or by outsiders. Elder statesmen of the group are likely to continue to identify strongly with it and hence to avoid exercising their judgmental faculties in relation to other members.

To understand the behavior of a group it is necessary to study the psychodynamic forces that bind the members of the group to its leader. The leader of any group—religious, judicial, industrial, political, or military—occupies a position in relation to the group which, from one angle of approach, seems not unlike that of parent to child.[1] Every individual is dimly aware that there was or is a person whose power and comfort he could rely on in times of dire necessity. It is not uncommon for an adult to encounter situations in which he feels helpless, much as he did during childhood, and longs for the omnipotent protection and comfort he feels he had when he was small. He obeys in order to be protected.[2] This feeling of dependency, common to all men, helps to bind the members of a group to their leader, causing them to acquiesce in his dictates.[3] It also strongly motivates them to rally around him even when his ability to lead may be impaired.

For proper psychiatric evaluation and treatment of VIPs there must be an understanding of the nature of communication and the extent to which this factor is relevant to the situation. Immunity from retaliation by both the patient and the official hierarchy must be assured if reasonable objectivity is to be attained. Privileged communication does not necessarily protect the physician from threat. Psychiatrists have found themselves threatened by

VIP patients for cooperating with other authorities and simultaneously criticized by the authorities for lack of cooperation. Thus it is particularly difficult for an examining psychiatrist to be objective in measuring impairment in any VIP who has, or is rumored to have, a psychiatric illness.

The VIP fears, and with good reason, that medical records may be used against him. The agency involved may wish to know the chance of recurrence, especially if the patient is paranoid, depressed, or alcoholic. In theory no need exists to release detailed confidential information. Unfortunately, however, confidentiality is frequently breached, as the VIP knows. His bias against psychiatric consultation, evaluation, and treatment therefore has a realistic as well as an emotional basis.

The same bias that makes an individual reluctant to place himself in the hands of a psychiatrist causes his associates to distrust him if he continues in office after it becomes known that he is or has been a psychiatric patient. Mental illness is viewed by the populace in general with fear and hostility. Psychological difficulties are regarded by some people as indicating moral weakness or defects of character. Many believe that treatment is vague and uncertain, that patients invariably deteriorate, and that the ultimate outlook is hopeless. Since mental illness is stigmatizing, it must be concealed. The mentally impaired VIP recognizes this and realizes that he is vulnerable. The inherent limitations of psychiatric prognosis contribute to the prevailing bias. Only recently has there been an attempt to understand how these concepts developed and why society has so little capacity to neutralize them.

six THE PSYCHIATRIST'S DILEMMA

The psychiatrist's professional encounter with the VIP is beset by difficulties at many levels.

The initial contact between the two is seldom arranged by a conventional medical referral. The VIP, because of his public position, influence, wealth, or perceived power, does not often seek psychiatric help voluntarily. His family is usually reluctant to reveal his aberrations for a variety of reasons—fear of the effect, of publicity, of decline in prestige, and so on. His superiors, peers, and subordinates discuss the problem furtively, usually in an atmosphere clouded by doubt and suspicion, and in this atmosphere may "approach" a psychiatrist.

Psychiatric referral of the VIP by the in-group, family, or subordinates may have sinister overtones which obscure the fact that he is a person, a human being in his own right, who may need psychiatric evaluation and care. Superiors may attempt to dodge their responsibilities by using the psychiatrist to remove an otherwise undesirable aide. Peers who may have self-seeking interests in direct competition with the VIP are necessarily suspect. Do they stand to gain by disclosure of the VIP's infirmity? Subordinates, on their part, may be envious, overtly or covertly hostile, too zealously protective, or vindictive.

These sources usually present a multitude of "valid" reasons why the VIP cannot be confronted directly with the suspected problem. A variety of devious plans for obtaining psychiatric evaluation are usually proposed. Sending the suspected mental patient to a neurologist is one of the milder gambits—mild, at least in comparison with some of the schemes that are contrived and occasionally carried out—for establishing contact between a VIP and a psychiatrist. Their initial contact with each other is almost invariably characterized by indirectness, doubt, and mistrust.

These gambits are rationalized and defended on the premise that the individual initiating the "referral" is subject to reprisal by the powerful patient. There is also unsureness and reluctance to be wrong, for the sake of both the referring person's own skin and the VIP's reputation, as well as because of a possible adverse effect on the morale of associates, staff, community, and nation. The VIP himself is often unaware of these interactions.

In some fortunate instances the initial contact is established in a more conventional fashion—for example, when the VIP patient is confronted with a colleague's concern about his health and is persuaded to see a private physician, or, if he is with an agency or a corporation, the organization's doctor, who may then be able to make a reasonably direct referral to a psychiatrist. But a psychiatrist who belongs to the official family or is on the staff of the corporation or the government agency may be reluctant about evaluating anyone with considerable ultimate control over the psychiatrist's own destiny. The dismissal of the director of a state hospital in Louisiana by Governor Long, already mentioned, is a prime example of what can happen when a psychiatrist attempts to diagnose the illness of "the boss," let alone to treat him.

Furthermore, the psychiatrist is frequently hamstrung by restrictions ranging from requests for secrecy and special meeting places to such outrageous demands as that the psychiatrist misrepresent himself or observe the potential patient surreptitiously. The psychiatrist must nevertheless evaluate all stipulations and conditions to determine which, if any, are appropriate and realistic in the case of the particular VIP he is asked to study professionally and to treat.

Clinical Evaluation

Problems surrounding the initial contact between psychiatrist and VIP patient extend into the clinical evaluation. Because referral information, obfuscated by doubt and mistrust, comes to the psychiatrist through devious channels, he must weigh it cautiously to avoid criticism from the leader's family and intimates, who may suspect the psychiatrist of being in league with his enemies.

On the one hand, there are demands for secrecy to protect the VIP, while, on the other, the public demands and even clamors for full information about its leader's health. He may try to shield himself behind a security cloak, and with high-level officials security restrictions may sometimes be partially justified. Essential, normally routine laboratory and psychological tests are performed only at the risk of increasing public knowledge of the leader's difficulties. The complexities of the clinical evaluation may be compounded if the psychiatrist has trouble in maintaining his own objectivity. The awe he feels toward the VIP patient he is examining may prevent him from being candid in his questioning, or his anxiety may diminish his clinical and professional acumen and objectivity and therefore his effectiveness.

Yet the psychiatrist must be concerned with his usual responsibilities to a patient. He must also be aware that in the case of high-ranking patients the need for confidentiality is absolute. Persons in public life are often reluctant or unwilling to seek help from a psychiatrist, even if they themselves feel the need, because they know that if the fact becomes known, they will be jeopardizing their careers or shaking the confidence of their public in their decisions and their leadership. The psychiatrist must nevertheless accept his responsibility not only to his patient but also to the organization, if industry is involved, or to the community and the national welfare, if the VIP is a public official. The problem of responsibility to patient versus responsibility to community may be even more difficult if clinical conditions are unclear, if data are concealed or distorted, or if the symptom picture is characterized by exacerbations and remissions.

Treatment Plans, Goals, and Strategies

After the psychiatrist has completed his clinical evaluation under what at best are difficult circumstances, he is likely to encounter additional problems in arranging for treatment that the VIP patient can accept. If the evaluation has been conducted officially for an agency or a corporation, the psychiatrist is usually obligated to report his findings to the referral source. How to disclose "public information" about the report is best left to the VIP and his official family. The psychiatrist is almost invariably under pressure to make a direct statement, but the fact that a question is asked does not by itself indicate that an answer is required.

Grave problems exist when the psychiatrist finds evidence of disabling psychopathology that raises questions about the VIP's competence to function in his position. The psychiatrist's responsibility to the patient as a human being and his obligations to the community depending upon the continued healthy functioning of the VIP are real. The psychiatrist must assess his patient's potential for therapy and consider treatment prospects in the light of whether the VIP should continue to work, be given a temporary leave of absence from official duties, or be relieved of them entirely. He must contend with the VIP's resistance to treatment and must recognize that the patient's protest usually has a realistic basis. Can the VIP afford, politically or within the corporate structure of industry, to be under psychiatric care? Furthermore, rigid schedules and heavy commitments make it difficult to schedule a regular program of psychiatric treatment. Even if intensive inpatient treatment is not indicated *per se,* it may nevertheless be necessary to remove the VIP from the setting that makes so many demands on his time and energy—or to remove him from his position of destructive influence. The latter decision is a social one to be made by those in appropriate positions.

Both inpatient and outpatient treatment programs for the VIP are complicated. The patient's personal and official families often present unreasonable demands. They are reluctant to cooperate or refuse to do so. They undoubtedly feel the anxiety that the image of a "fallen idol" creates. Public pressures for information and for access to the patient begin before the moment of initial contact and continue throughout the period of treatment.

There remain still further barriers to providing optimum care for the VIP patient. The emotional responses of the psychiatrist and his co-workers to the VIP must be resolved to provide for the best treatment. Special, usually poor compromises must often be made when distinguished patients are treated. In the case of King Ludwig, the psychiatrist's apparent failure to take the usual precautions for a paranoid patient may have caused the death of both psychiatrist and patient. Similar pressures, exceptions, and variance from the usual routine contributed to the suicide of James Forrestal. Treatment programs may be so complicated by exceptions and special considerations as to preclude optimal measures.

Furthermore, the psychiatrist who makes an honest effort to provide the best possible medical care for his distinguished patient can expect to be bombarded by telephone calls, letters, and visits from relatives, co-workers, other VIPs, and the press. He is forced at times to yield to these pressures, at least to some extent, in order to keep his patient under treatment.

Through fear of loss of status and position, as well as for other reasons, many VIPs conceal their identity while under treatment. It is difficult to treat a VIP in a community where he is well known.

A prominent and universally respected psychiatrist in Washington, D.C., reported that in his long experience he had never been able to maintain a member of Congress in treatment for more than a few months. He concluded that it was not possible in that setting.

At times patients do not wish to consult a psychiatrist employed by their own organization, either because they doubt the direction of the psychiatrist's loyalties, or because they do not wish to have purely personal material, such as disclosures about family life, noted in organizational medical records. On the other hand, financial difficulties may militate against their seeking private psychiatric care. The increasing prevalence of major medical insurance may ameliorate this problem, but major insurance coverers have also attempted to obtain confidential information about psychiatric patients.

Completing a treatment program successfully does not necessarily end the problems of dealing with the VIP patient. In some instances, the psychiatrist then has the task of convincing the public or the official family that the patient has recovered and is fit to reassume his duties. The fact that an individual has undergone psychiatric treatment is in itself still stigmatizing in many quarters.

seven CONCLUSIONS AND RECOMMENDATIONS

THE COMMITTEE'S STUDY of the issues and problems presented in this report has led to the following conclusions:

1. Organized psychiatry should approach government representatives and agencies on a purely consultative basis, making known to significant members what can and cannot be done with present psychiatric and psychologic knowledge to cope with the mentally impaired VIP in public life.
2. Those who attend the VIP should have certain specific qualities of personality and character. They should be professionally highly competent, beyond professional and personal reproach, clearly not self-seeking, free of political and administrative involvement, and imbued with the moral courage needed to take and maintain a position. In short, their qualities and attributes should tend to enable them to be objective and immune to pressure.
3. Great care is necessary at all echelons of government to avoid unbidden and unwarranted prying into the personal

lives of its workers. Complaints reaching high governmental levels about ill-advised psychiatric and psychologic test inquiries have resulted in subsequent interference with needed psychiatric programs. Public knowledge of psychiatric inquiry is currently considered the kiss of death to a high-level official.

4. A well-publicized practice of seeking an annual complete physical examination would make it possible for the VIP to consult his private physician or to be admitted to a clinic or hospital without undue public comment. When a physician has identified a mental or physical disorder that has impaired a high official's functioning as a leader, a pre-existing mechanism must be available to recommend action. Panels of internists, surgeons, and psychiatrists, carefully preselected by the appropriate professional organizations, should be provided to conduct examinations of VIPs on request.

The committee recommends that organized psychiatry make continuing and unremitting efforts to accomplish the following:

1. Educate high-level figures in the administration and organization, alerting them to signs, symptoms, and conditions of psychiatric impairment.
2. Provide in advance channels for dealing with problems as they arise.
3. Provide that each agency, branch, and the like, have ready access to a qualified psychiatrist familiar with its special problems.
4. Inform both the participant psychiatrist and the VIP's superiors (who will be dealing with the VIP when and if he

becomes a patient) of problems uniquely associated with his psychiatric condition.

5. Provide, when treatment begins, acceptable channels for communicating with the originating organization without violating competent patient confidentiality.
6. Make available to any requesting governmental agency a panel of qualified psychiatrists, designated by the American Psychiatric Association, which should be appointed on a permanent rather than on an ad hoc basis. Provision should be made for rotation of members, and they should have security clearance at the time of appointment. This panel would be immediately available to provide examination, consultation, and psychiatric recommendation in the event that a question of the inability of the President of the United States arises under the Twenty-fifth Amendment to the Constitution of the United States (see Appendix).

APPENDIX

REFERENCE NOTES

INDEX

APPENDIX

The Twenty-fifth Amendment to the Constitution of the United States

Section 1. In case of the removal of the President from office or of his death or resignation, the Vice President shall become President.

Section 2. Whenever there is a vacancy in the office of the Vice President, the President shall nominate a Vice President who shall take office upon confirmation by a majority vote of both Houses of Congress.

Section 3. Whenever the President transmits to the President pro tempore of the Senate and the Speaker of the House of Representatives his written declaration that he is unable to discharge the powers and duties of his office, and until he transmits to them a written declaration to the contrary, such powers and duties shall be discharged by the Vice President as Acting President.

Section 4. Whenever the Vice President and a majority of either the principal officers of the executive departments or of such other body as Congress may by law provide, transmit to the President pro tempore of the Senate and the Speaker of the House of Representatives their written declaration that the President is unable to discharge the powers and duties of his office, the Vice President shall immediately assume the powers and duties of the Office as Acting President.

Thereafter, when the President transmits to the President pro tempore of the Senate and the Speaker of the House of Representatives his written declaration that no inability exists, he shall resume the powers and duties of his office unless the Vice President and a majority of either the principal officers of the executive department or of such other body as Congress may by law provide, transmit within four days to the President pro tempore of the Senate and the Speaker of the House of Representatives their written declaration that the President is unable to discharge the powers and duties of his office. Thereupon Congress shall decide the issue, assembling within forty-eight hours for that purpose if not in session. If the Congress, within twenty-one days after receipt of the latter written declaration, or, if Congress is not in session, within twenty-one days after Congress is required to assemble, determines by a two-thirds vote of both Houses that the President is unable to discharge the powers and duties of his office, the Vice President shall continue to discharge the same as Acting President; otherwise, the President shall resume the powers and duties of his office.

REFERENCE NOTES

one • The VIP and the Psychiatrist

1. Ernest Barker, *The Politics of Aristotle* (New York: Oxford University Press, 1946).
2. Richard Collier, *Duce* (New York: The Viking Press, 1971).
3. Hugh L'Etang, *The Pathology of Leadership* (New York: Hawthorn Books, 1970), chapter 15, "Statesmen and Their Doctors: Quis Custodiet Ipsos Custodes?"

two • Emotionally Ill VIPs in History

1. Manfred S. Guttmacher, *America's Last King* (New York: Charles Scribner's Sons, 1941); McAlpine and Hunter, *The Insanity of King George III: A Classic Case of Porphyria* (London: British Medical Association, 1968).
2. Wilfred Blount, *The Dream King: Ludwig II of Bavaria* (London: Hamish Hamilton, Ltd., 1970).
3. Leo Alexander, "The Commitment and Suicide of King Ludwig of Bavaria," *American Journal of Psychiatry*, 110:100–107, 1954.
4. Barbara W. Tuchman, *The Guns of August* (New York: Dell Publishing Co., paperback, 1963), pp. 344–345.

5. William L. Shirer, *The Rise and Fall of the Third Reich* (New York: Simon and Schuster, 1960), p. 163.
6. For further details, see L'Etang, *The Pathology of Leadership*, chapter 3, "Admirals and Generals, 1914–18: No Miracle at the Marne."
7. Curt Reiss, *Joseph Goebbels* (New York: Ballantine Books, 1960), p. 115.
8. Edith Bolling Wilson, *My Memoirs* (Indianapolis: Bobbs-Merrill Co., 1939), quoted in American Bar Association, Washington Letter, July 9, 1965, "Presidential Inability and Vice-Presidential Vacancy."
9. Edwin A. Weinstein, "Denial of Presidential Disability: A Case Study of Woodrow Wilson," *Psychiatry*, 30:376–391, 1967; Gene Smith, *When the Cheering Stopped: The Last Years of Woodrow Wilson* (New York: Willam Morrow & Co., 1964).
10. Cary Grayson, *Woodrow Wilson: An Intimate Memoir* (New York: Henry Holt & Co., 1960).
11. William C. Bullitt, "How We Won the War and Lost the Peace," Part Two, *Life*, Vol. 25, No. 10, September 6, 1948, p. 86.
12. John Gunther, *Roosevelt in Retrospect* (New York: Harper & Brothers, 1950), p. 360.
13. Winston Spencer Churchill, *The Second World War: Triumph and Tragedy* (Boston: Houghton Mifflin Co., 1953), pp. 419; 344–383.
14. *Ibid.*, p. 455.
15. Robert Murphy, *Diplomat Among Warriors* (New York: Doubleday and Co., 1964).
16. Ross T. McIntire, *White House Physician* (New York: G. P. Putnam's Sons, 1946).
17. Howard G. Bruenn, "Clinical Notes on the Illness and Death of President Franklin D. Roosevelt," *Annals of Internal Medicine*, 72:579–591, 1970.
18. James M. Burns, "FDR: The Untold Story of His Last Year," *Saturday Review*, April 11, 1970, p. 13.
19. Lester Grinspoon, "The Decision Makers' Dilemma," *Harvard Medical Bulletin*, Summer, 1964.
20. *Ibid.*
21. Dr. Cattabeni described his gross findings in C. M. Cattabeni,

"Rendiconto di una Necropsia d'Eccezione," *Clinica Nuova*, 1:3–5, August 1945.

22. Letter of January 28, 1946, from Calvin S. Drayer, M.D., to Winfred Overholzer, M.D., Superintendent, St. Elizabeths Hospital, Washington, D.C.
23. Letter of June 12, 1962, from Earl T. Crain, American Consul General, Milan, Italy, to Calvin S. Drayer, M.D.

three • Problems of Coping with Mental Impairment

1. "The Truth About Governor Earl K. Long," *The American Weekly*, September 20, 1959.
2. A. A. Rogow, "Disability in High Office," *Medical Opinion and Review*, 1:16–19, 1966.
3. Herman Wouk, *The Caine Mutiny* (New York: Doubleday and Co., 1954); William Bligh, *Mutiny on Board H.M.S. Bounty* (London: Airmont and Signal, [n.d.])
4. Harold Rosen and H. Kiene, "The Paranoiac Officer and the Officer Paranee," *American Journal of Psychiatry*, 103:614–621, 1947.
5. J. E. Frankel, "Removal of Judges: California Tackles an Old Problem," *Journal of the American Bar Association*, 49:166–171, 1963.
6. *Ibid.*

five • Significant Aspects of the VIP Situation

1. Sigmund Freud, *Group Psychology and the Analysis of the Ego*, Vol. 18, The Standard Edition of the Complete Works of Sigmund Freud (London: Hogarth Press, 1955).
2. Otto Fenichel, *Psychoanalytic Theory of Neurosis* (New York: W. W. Norton and Co., 1945), pp. 491–492.
3. Franz Alexander, *Our Age of Unreason* (Philadelphia: J. P. Lippincott Co., 1942), p. 250.

INDEX

GAP COMMITTEES, MEMBERS, AND OFFICERS
(as of July 1, 1972)

COMMITTEES

ADOLESCENCE
Joseph D. Noshpitz, Washington, D.C., *Chairman*
Warren J. Gadpaille, Englewood, Colo.
Charles A. Malone, Philadelphia, Pa.
Silvio J. Onesti, Jr., Boston, Mass.
Jeanne Spurlock, Nashville, Tenn.
Sidney L. Werkman, Denver, Colo.

AGING
Robert N. Butler, Washington, D.C., *Chairman*
Charles M. Gaitz, Houston, Tex.
Alvin I. Goldfarb, New York, N.Y.
Lawrence F. Greenleigh, Los Angeles, Calif.
Maurice E. Linden, Philadelphia, Pa.
Prescott W. Thompson, San Jose, Calif.
Montague Ullman, Brooklyn, N.Y.
Jack Weinberg, Chicago, Ill.

CHILD PSYCHIATRY
E. James Anthony, St. Louis, Mo., *Chairman*
James M. Bell, Canaan, N.Y.
Harlow Donald Dunton, New York, N.Y.
Joseph M. Green, Tucson, Ariz.
John F. Kenward, Chicago, Ill.
John F. McDermott, Jr., Honolulu, Hawaii
Exie E. Welsch, New York, N.Y.
Virginia N. Wilking, New York, N.Y.

THE COLLEGE STUDENT
Robert L. Arnstein, New Haven, Conn., *Chairman*
Harrison P. Eddy, New York, N.Y.
Malkah Tolpin Notman, Brookline, Mass.
Kent E. Robinson, Towson, Md.
Earle Silber, Chevy Chase, Md.
Tom G. Stauffer, White Plains, N.Y.

THE FAMILY
David Mendell, Houston, Tex., *Chairman*
C. Christian Beels, New York, N.Y.
Ivan Boszormenyi-Nagy, Philadelphia, Pa.
Murray Bowen, Chevy Chase, Md.

Henry U. Grunebaum, Boston, Mass.
Margaret M. Lawrence, Pomona, N.Y.
Henry D. Lederer, Washington, D.C.
Norman L. Paul, Cambridge, Mass.
Joseph Satten, San Francisco, Calif.
Kurt O. Schlesinger, San Francisco, Calif.
Israel Zwerling, New York, N.Y.

GOVERNMENTAL AGENCIES

Paul Chodoff, Washington, D.C., *Chairman*
William S. Allerton, Richmond, Va.
Albert M. Biele, Philadelphia, Pa.
John E. Nardini, Washington, D.C.
Donald B. Peterson, Fulton, Mo.
Harvey L. P. Resnick, Chevy Chase, Md.
Harold Rosen, Baltimore, Md.

INTERNATIONAL RELATIONS

Byrant M. Wedge, San Diego, Calif., *Chairman*
Francis F. Barnes, Chevy Chase, Md.
Eric A. Baum, Cambridge, Mass.
Eugene B. Brody, Baltimore, Md.
William D. Davidson, Washington, D.C.
Alexander Gralnick, Port Chester, N.Y.
Robert L. Leopold, Philadelphia, Pa.
Rita R. Rogers, Torrance, Calif.
Bertram H. Schaffner, New York, N.Y.
Mottram P. Torre, New Orleans, La.
Ronald M. Wintrob, Hartford, Conn.

MEDICAL EDUCATION

David R. Hawkins, Charlottesville, Va., *Chairman*
Robert S. Daniels, Chicago, Ill.
Raymond Feldman, Boulder, Colo.
Saul I. Harrison, Ann Arbor, Mich.
Harold I. Lief, Philadelphia, Pa.
John E. Mack, Boston, Mass.
William L. Peltz, Longview, Vt.
David S. Sanders, Los Angeles, Calif.
Robert A. Senescu, Albuquerque, N. Mex.
Roy M. Whitman, Cincinnati, Ohio

MENTAL HEALTH SERVICES

Merrill T. Eaton, Omaha, Nebr., *Chairman*
Allan Beigel, Tucson, Ariz.
H. Keith H. Brodie, Menlo Park, Calif.
Eugene M. Caffey, Jr., Washington, D.C.
Archie R. Foley, New York, N.Y.
James B. Funkhouser, Richmond, Va.
Robert S. Garber, Belle Mead, N.J.
Stanley Hammons, Frankfort, Ky.
Alan I. Levenson, Tucson, Ariz.
W. Walter Menninger, Topeka, Kans.
Donald Scherl, Boston, Mass.
Percy C. Talkington, Dallas, Tex.
Jack A. Wolford, Pittsburgh, Pa.

MENTAL RETARDATION

Henry H. Work, Washington, D.C., *Chairman*
Howard V. Bair, Parsons, Kans.
Stuart M. Finch, Ann Arbor, Mich.
Leo Madow, Philadelphia, Pa.
George Tarjan, Los Angeles, Calif.
Warren T. Vaughan, Jr., Burlingame, Calif.
Thomas G. Webster, Chevy Chase, Md.

PREVENTIVE PSYCHIATRY

Stephen Fleck, New Haven, Conn., *Chairman*
Frederick Gottlieb, Sherman Oaks, Calif.

Benjamin Jeffries, Harper Woods, Mich.
Ruth W. Lidz, Woodbridge, Conn.
E. James Lieberman, Washington, D.C.
Mary E. Mercer, Nyack, N.Y.
Harris B. Peck, New York, N.Y.
Marvin E. Perkins, Mamaroneck, N.Y.
Harold M. Visotsky, Chicago, Ill.

PSYCHIATRY AND LAW
Alan A. Stone, Cambridge, Mass., *Chairman*
Edward T. Auer, St. Louis, Mo.
John Donnelly, Hartford, Conn.
Carl P. Malmquist, Minneapolis, Minn.
A. Louis McGarry, Brookline, Mass.
Seymour Pollack, Los Angeles, Calif.
Gene L. Usdin, New Orleans, La.

PSYCHIATRY AND RELIGION
Sidney S. Furst, New York, N.Y., *Chairman*
Stanley A. Leavy, New Haven, Conn.
Richard C. Lewis, New Haven, Conn.
Earl A. Loomis, Jr., New York, N.Y.
Albert J. Lubin, Woodside, Calif.
Mortimer Ostow, New York, N.Y.
Bernard L. Pacella, New York, N.Y.

PSYCHIATRY AND SOCIAL WORK
John A. MacLeod, Cincinnati, Ohio, *Chairman*
C. Knight Aldrich, Newark, N.J.
Maurice R. Friend, New York, N.Y.
Herbert C. Modlin, Topeka, Kans.
John C. Nemiah, Boston, Mass.
Alexander S. Rogawski, Los Angeles, Calif.

Charles B. Wilkinson, Kansas City, Mo.

PSYCHIATRY IN INDUSTRY
Clarence J. Rowe, St. Paul, Minn., *Chairman*
Spencer Bayles, Houston, Tex.
Thomas L. Brannick, Imola, Calif.
Duane Q. Hagen, St. Louis, Mo.
R. Edward Huffman, Asheville, N.C.
Herbert L. Klemme, Topeka, Kans.
Alan A. McLean, New York, N.Y.
David E. Morrison, Topeka, Kans.
John Wakefield, Cambridge, Mass.

PSYCHOPATHOLOGY
George E. Ruff, Philadelphia, Pa., *Chairman*
Wagner H. Bridger, New York, N.Y.
Sanford I. Cohen, Boston, Mass.
Daniel X. Freedman, Chicago, Ill.
Paul E. Huston, Iowa City, Iowa
Jack H. Mendelson, Boston, Mass.
Richard E. Renneker, Los Angeles, Calif.
Charles Shagass, Philadelphia, Pa.
Albert J. Silverman, Ann Arbor, Mich.
George E. Vaillant, Boston, Mass.

PUBLIC EDUCATION
Miles F. Shore, Boston, Mass., *Chairman*
Leo H. Bartemeier, Baltimore, Md.
Robert J. Campbell, New York, N.Y.
James A. Knight, New Orleans, La.
John P. Lambert, Katonah, N.Y.
Norman L. Loux, Sellersville, Pa.
Peter A. Martin, Smithfield, Mich.
Mildred Mitchell-Bateman, Charleston, S.C.
Mabel Ross, Atlanta, Ga.
Julius Schreiber, Washington, D.C.
Robert H. Sharpley, Brookline, Mass.

Robert A. Solow, Beverly Hills, Calif.

Kent A. Zimmerman, Berkeley, Calif.

RESEARCH

Morris A. Lipton, Chapel Hill, N.C., *Chairman*

Stanley E. Eldred, Belmont, Mass.

Louis A. Gottschalk, Irvine, Calif.

Donald F. Klein, Glen Oaks, N.Y.

Gerald L. Klerman, Boston, Mass.

Ralph R. Notman, Brookline, Mass.

Alfred H. Stanton, Belmont, Mass.

Eberhard H. Uhlenhuth, Chicago, Ill.

SOCIAL ISSUES

Kendon W. Smith, Piermont, N.Y., *Chairman*

Viola W. Bernard, New York, N.Y.

Lester Grinspoon, Boston, Mass.

Joel S. Handler, Evanston, Ill.

Judd Marmor, Los Angeles, Calif.

Roy W. Menninger, Topeka, Kans.

Peter B. Neubauer, New York, N.Y.

Perry Ottenberg, Philadelphia, Pa.

Charles A. Pinderhughes, Boston, Mass.

THERAPEUTIC CARE

Robert W. Gibson, Towson, Md., *Chairman*

Bernard Bandler, Chevy Chase, Md.

Ian L. W. Clancey, Ottawa, Canada

Thomas E. Curtis, Chapel Hill, N.C.

Harold A. Greenberg, Bethesda, Md.

Milton Kramer, Cincinnati, Ohio

Orlando B. Lightfoot, Brookline, Mass.

Melvin Sabshin, Chicago, Ill.

Robert E. Switzer, Topeka, Kans.

THERAPY

Peter H. Knapp, Boston, Mass., *Chairman*

Henry W. Brosin, Tucson, Ariz.

Eugene Meyer, Baltimore, Md.

William C. Offenkrantz, Chicago, Ill.

Franz K. Reichsman, Brooklyn, N.Y.

Lewis L. Robbins, Glen Oaks, N.Y.

Richard E. Shader, Newton Center, Mass.

Harley C. Shands, New York, N.Y.

Justin Simon, Berkeley, Calif.

Herbert Weiner, Stanford, Calif.

MEMBERS

CONTRIBUTING MEMBERS

Marvin L. Adland, Chevy Chase, Md.

Carlos C. Alden, Jr., Buffalo, N.Y.

William H. Anderson, Lansing, Mich.

Kenneth E. Appel, Ardmore, Pa.

M. Royden C. Astley, Pittsburgh, Pa.

Charlotte G. Babcock, Pittsburgh, Pa.

Grace Baker, New York, N.Y.

Walter E. Barton, Washington, D.C.

Anne R. Benjamin, Chicago, Ill.

Ivan C. Berlien, Coral Gables, Fla.

Sidney Berman, Washington, D.C.

Grete L. Bibring, Cambridge, Mass.

Edward G. Billings, Denver, Colo.

Carl A. L. Binger, Cambridge, Mass.

H. Waldo Bird, St. Louis, Mo.

Wilfred Bloomberg, Hartford, Conn.

Peter W. Bowman, Pownal, Maine

Matthew Brody, Brooklyn, N.Y.

Ewald W. Busse, Durham, N.C.

Dale C. Cameron, Geneva, Switzerland

Norman Cameron, Tucson, Ariz.

Gerald Caplan, Boston, Mass.
Hugh T. Carmichael, Washington, D.C.
Morris E. Chafetz, Rockville, Md.
Jules V. Coleman, New Haven, Conn.
Robert Coles, Cambridge, Mass.
Harvey H. Corman, New York, N.Y.
Frank J. Curran, New York, N.Y.
Leonard J. Duhl, Berkeley, Calif.
Lloyd C. Elam, Nashville, Tenn.
Joel Elkes, Baltimore, Md.
Joseph T. English, New York, N.Y.
Louis C. English, Pomona, N.Y.
O. Spurgeon English, Narbeth, Pa.
Jack R. Ewalt, Boston, Mass.
James H. Ewing, Wallingford, Pa.
Dana L. Farnsworth, Boston, Mass.
Malcolm J. Farrell, Waverley, Mass.
Alfred Flarsheim, Chicago, Ill.
Alan Frank, Albuquerque, N. Mex.
Edward C. Frank, Louisville, Ky.
Lawrence Z. Freedman, Chicago, Ill.
Frank Fremont-Smith, Massapequa, N.Y.
Moses M. Frohlich, Ann Arbor, Mich.
Daniel H. Funkenstein, Boston, Mass.
Albert J. Glass, Chicago, Ill.
Milton Greenblatt, Boston, Mass.
Maurice H. Greenhill, Scarsdale, N.Y.
John H. Greist, Indianapolis, Ind.
Roy R. Grinker, Sr., Chicago, Ill.
Ernest M. Gruenberg, Poughkeepsie, N.Y.
Edward O. Harper, Washington, D.C.
Mary O'Neill Hawkins, New York, N.Y.
J. Cotter Hirschberg, Topeka, Kans.
Edward J. Hornick, New York, N.Y.
Joseph Hughes, Philadelphia, Pa.
Portia Bell Hume, Berkeley, Calif.
Lucie Jessner, Washington, D.C.
Irene M. Josselyn, Phoenix, Ariz.
Jay Katz, New Haven, Conn.
Sheppard G. Kellam, Chicago, Ill.
Marion E. Kenworthy, New York, N.Y.
Ernest W. Klatte, Santa Ana, Calif.
Othilda M. Krug, Cincinnati, Ohio
Zigmond M. Lebensohn, Washington, D.C.
P. Herbert Leiderman, Palo Alto, Calif.
David M. Levy, New York, N.Y.
Robert J. Lifton, Woodbridge, Conn.
Reginald S. Lourie, Washington, D.C.
Alfred O. Ludwig, Boston, Mass.
Jeptha R. MacFarlane, Westbury, N.Y.
Helen V. McLean, Chicago, Ill.
Sydney G. Margolin, Denver, Colo.
Karl A. Menninger, Topeka, Kans.
James G. Miller, Washington, D.C.
John A. P. Millet, New York, N.Y.
Kenneth J. Munden, Memphis, Tenn.
Rudolph G. Novick, Lincolnwood, Ill.
Lucy D. Ozarin, Bethesda, Md.
Irving Philips, San Francisco, Calif.
Vivian Rakoff, Toronto, Canada
Eveoleen N. Rexford, Cambridge, Mass.
Milton Rosenbaum, New York, N.Y.
W. Donald Ross, Cincinnati, Ohio
Lester H. Rudy, Chicago, Ill.
Elvin V. Semrad, Boston, Mass.
Calvin F. Settlage, Sausalito, Calif.
Benson R. Snyder, Cambridge, Mass.
John P. Spiegel, Waltham, Mass.